Little Wildheart

THE UNIVERSITY OF ALBERTA PRESS

Little Wildheart

MICHELINE MAYLOR

Published by

The University of Alberta Press
Ring House 2
Edmonton, Alberta, Canada T6G 2E1
www.uap.ualberta.ca

LIBRARY AND ARCHIVES CANADA
CATALOGUING IN PUBLICATION

Maylor, Micheline, 1970–, author
Little wildheart / Micheline Maylor.

(Robert Kroetsch series)
Issued in print and electronic formats.
ISBN 978-1-77212-233-6 (paperback).–
ISBN 978-1-77212-316-6 (EPUB).–
ISBN 978-1-77212-317-3 (kindle).–
ISBN 978-1-77212-318-0 (PDF)

I. Title. II. Series: Robert Kroetsch series

PS8626.A9328L58 2017 C811'.6
C2016-907317-3

First edition, first printing, 2017.
First printed and bound in Canada by Houghton Boston Printers, Saskatoon, Saskatchewan.
Copyediting and proofreading by Peter Midgley.

A volume in the Robert Kroetsch Series.

The University of Alberta Press is committed to protecting our natural environment. As part of our efforts, this book is printed on Enviro Paper: it contains 100% post-consumer recycled fibres and is acid- and chlorine-free.

The University of Alberta Press gratefully acknowledges the support received for its publishing program from the Government of Canada, the Canada Council for the Arts, and the Government of Alberta through the Alberta Media Fund.

Canada Canada Council for the Arts Conseil des Arts du Canada

Alberta Government

For Ava

You must live by the dream
However strange the dream

—TOM MARSHALL

Contents

We are entirely flammable

Come, walk an open road. Stand.
Meld a hawk's shadow
with your own. Note
wing-tips spark-spread
out of yourself and up. Feel
fire in your thighs, your thighs and lungs, as you run
daily towards your own cremation. Know
the purification in this act. See
with all clarity, and from way up,
what the predator knows:
Death already hunts.

Autobiography

If the temperature would hold, I'd stay for hours seduced by summer light
west heat, where life spends itself on visions of skimming water, rock, light.

Airwaves fill with classic rock, gull and hawk, corona of sun. Moments
become vivid, condense, ice water on the warm other side. Moments

as droplets of love. Yes. Let's say we can know those moments only
by the trial of time, by heat, by flat black rocks skipping, only

skimming, on moments and only through light.

Convergence

The long strand of my DNA casts its blood shape
back to snow, a spattered deer-kill, the struck life
narrowing to strips of pemmican in some voyageur's pouch.

Somewhere else my DNA sits near the beach of Loch Lomond,
watches ice floes in afternoon light afire with chill-spark and halo.

Yet another strand of DNA plants wheat and lilac near
Troglodyte caves, evening indigo high in the stratosphere
peppered with faraway suns, reproducing lustrous blossoms below.

Tiny epiphanies ladder. Double-stranded ascensions to past and sky.
This is to say, my life is a hallway between those strands.

This is to say, no one is defined by space or time.
This is to say, I declare my citizenship to the sun.

Light travels 150 million kilometres without bias,
or prejudice, or ownership of anywhere, or anyone.

The lovers

Three robins animate the bush,
release a shrill, and bit of fusty bark
after a skirmish of leaf and flung feather.
Two males and a female wrestle–
trill, a triangular aubade
of swoop and peck,
squawk and plunder.
Oh, girl!

Those blows will
build you now
a nest of blue ovals,
a fate of hungry crows.
I cannot call it love.

Dissilience

On the only curve in the straight road,
the white Jeep Cherokee ploughed a furrow,
sowed rodents into graves. They bloomed in the zenith
that May afternoon, their secret parts
all gravel and oracle. They blossomed up
and asked sunlight with their last breath,
What should I have become?

The sun yawned a solar flare,
answered, *just do it with guts.*

And the gophers, whose life had already faded,
opened their ribs, peony-like, wild, unclenched.
And the opossum cracked her skull, a burst seedpod,
flowered a puddle of brain and kidney on asphalt.

Then they unwound tendrils of intestines up to the sky
and offered organs to heaven above
with all the bravery they could.

Ten

You are ten years old and come home from school.

Your dad tells you to read the encyclopaedia from the start to the end for an hour every day.

You hate him for a minute, realize the futility of this hatred and begin at Aardvark, Abyssal Fish, while your friends play Kick-the-Can and watch reruns of Dudley Do-Right on tiny black and white televisions.

A friend of your mother's comes over.

She is French and decorative in clothes and speech.

She says you are provincial and daft, but somehow she is kind with her disdain, a study in contrasts.

Later, years later, your husband, of whom she does not approve, will shoot a champagne cork through her meticulous hair, narrowly missing her refined forehead, and somehow he will make her laugh about the gaffe.

You know you love him in that moment; his ability to make everything calm, even the French tiger-woman who has somehow found herself stranded on the prairie where the weather is hard and the artichokes are impossible and all the men are cowboys with bad manners.

But time is moving on, ticking off each complaint, and she will disappear on her own terms, calling your mother whatever she needs to–to get out of the friendship, to stop calling.

And she will live in London where there is culture, art, and food from the cornucopia of God himself.

And your mother will cry. She will spill her ribs open to look at her broken heart like a clockmaker, pulling apart the workings to understand why.

Every part looks perfect, but still she seeks reasons.

But this wasn't about your mother or her friend, it was about you, the way the world shapes you incrementally, the way words define you.

And sometimes now, when you play Scrabble with your husband, you think of how love means you hold each other accountable, because you only read to M, to Marriage, before your father left, and you are very good at Scrabble for only half the alphabet, because time ran out when you least expected it and you just weren't old enough to make yourself finish anything and maybe that French woman was right, you are completely daft, but maybe she's wrong.

There *is* a way of making a good score out of a rack of Ns and Os if only you work hard enough, look long enough.

There must be a way, a word, an explanation, a reason.

In Saskatchewan, surrealism invades the silence

Twelve televisions play in my tiny room. Each one projects a face
of someone loved and dead. Each one says something they forgot to
remember to tell me. Each day, I am allowed to turn one television off.

After all, this is a retreat: silence is golden,
even the otherworld must hush.

Something about the rules here I don't understand. A clause about
time and perception–I missed the fine print, its confusing conclusions.
Damn those applications.

I leave the voices on–talking all the time, a cacophony of hums. I've
missed my grandmother's face more than the rest. Her television is on
mute, but I watch her lips, the way we have the same Cupid's bow.

Birds outside speak a language I can't comprehend. Their throat song
is meant to explain the purpose of life, my life. I make out that it is
sweet sweet sweet.

I do luxurious things after dinner and wine: *I think therefore*...what?
I thought?

The whole province spins lazy Susan in the middle of the country. A
clock with a minute hand running down with a wonky battery
all positives and negatives are shape-shifted, sublime.

Something about all of this is important. I don't know why.
I am born as a chick, sun-shocked, blind.

Rewind

The girl is safe, tucked in her bed.
5:30 am when she crumpled there.
Her torn skirt lay bare in the garbage.
The lost shoes weren't good ones anyway.

4:30am when she finally walked
from that boy's party.
The lost shoes weren't good ones anyway.
She woke her mother with a story in the night

from the boy's party.
She said, *I'm home now.*
She woke her mother with a story of the night,
A man chased me down the street.

She's home now.
His grip was on her skirt and he pulled.
A man chased her down the street
until her hem ripped up to the waistband.

His hand was on her skirt and he pulled
until she fell on a doorstep and rang and rang
until the hem ripped up to the waistband.
She pounded and pounded and pounded and pounded

until she fell on a doorstep and rang and rang.
Nobody came.
She pounded and pounded and pounded and pounded.
No, she doesn't want to phone the police. It's late.

Nobody came
and what would they do, anyway, that hasn't been done?
No, I don't want to phone the police. It's too late.
I am so tired, mum.

And what would they do that hasn't already been done?
Her torn skirt is in the garbage
and she is so tired.
The girl is safe, tucked in her bed.

Rust

She spent a lot of her time
preparing for a cushy fall, or an afternoon lay
stacking the mattresses in her favour
for a naked prince with cascading locks and a donkey
cock to stench up her blankets.
She wanted her hair to fan mermaid style, have sheets
of silk soft as sea foam. She wanted her days bracketed
by a mile high bed filled with the down of Zeus' geese.
She wanted it all, but she saved in her pocket a secret so small,
a rusted pellet from a blacksmith's shop, a top of a hobnail
for slipping under those tickings
when things got too tricky.
Every princess always needs a good complaint,
a little pea to rely on.

Conscientious objectors

She's learning to lie, in this car, right now, and to swear, too,
by the light of a taillight and its unannounced lane shift.
She's learning to take what her teacher says by half, to use
her own common sense. She's learning that skipping school
for the sake of catching something amazing like the science fair
at university, the opera, fireworks, something educational and wise,
has its consequences. She's learning to read ingredients, read
between the lines, that the FDA lies. She's learning about the man
on Wall Street who wants all the money, a leprechaun
named Gold-Wallet, the ways he'll trick her with glitter, electronics,
and buzz. She's learning about those men, their entertainment,
the Humberts of the world. She's learning to run. She's learning
double-speak, the slippery way of the word, the words,
the well-worded, the wisely worded, the way of the word,
the first word, the last word, about holding her tongue.
She's learning ignorance is bliss, that sometimes even I am tongue-tied.
She's learning that I could make it easier on her, easier on me, more blissful,
in this car, right now, by telling her a pretty lie. But I won't.

Polarity

Child, your axis spins fast as your mood,
but tonight you are fond of me.
The you you become sometimes
when you forget to be uppity.
Stretched out on the carpet
on my friend's living room,
our talk of grown-up things
perks your hungry ears in hope
of hearing an adult secret,
a way past your child body,
its limitations.

You cover more floor than I
recall from the last time we were here.
Your nipples have swollen,
itchy fruit beneath your puppy-dog tee-shirt.
I watch you tip-toe back to the kitchen
for a third slice of velvet cake, answering only
your body's constant whimper to be fed.

In the doorframe, that cusp
between two worlds,
you pirouette.
The twirl of your woman skin
hasn't slowed you.
Not yet.

Before the dark

Its penciled pages a Rosetta stone.
A daughter forgets her diary.
Home from school today
the little book calls to me.

Holds the language of the other.
On the cover, sun breaks the spell:
A mother must set herself beyond
desire for secrets, beyond the thrill

of necessary gravity between them, like planets.
Sun must slink darkward before the clock
tells a story that begins with the words,
a mother has betrayed her child, her lock.

Morning on the old reserve

Hieroglyphs of impermanence tell a story
writ by tidal ebbs scribbled on the shore-line.
The imperfect bind of *happened one time* and *recall*.

Shapes and faces morph, loose as toe-tipped
mushroom caps, in union with autumn leaves.
I hear you, ancestor, across the dark water.

Your low French speaking my name
through your pointed Coyote teeth,
your Roman nose. My ears listen

for our history. Speak clearly,
the fog is so thick this morning.

Detroit Zoo bathroom 1977

"Hey, Nigger, Where'd you get that kid?"

Pale as an anaemic and holding hands with a goddess,
I learned the word racist in the grip of my grandmother.
Bronzed Queen of the Huron, mixed-breed, multi-lingual,
lady of St. Clair lake, she tanned dark as curses.
Me, bleached to blend in Prairie snow, white as a winter hare,
hadn't yet moulted into my golden summer skin. Photoperiodism
not yet complete. Call it too much Anglo-breeding
with fair-haired men. Call it what you will,
call it nights in my teenage years
asking my brown eyes and black hair: why?
Only one Mattel Barbie coloured like me, unglamorously named Skipper.
Skip her. Where is my blonde hair, my Sun-In, my glacial eyes?
I check the box on the government forms: Caucasian. No box
for colonized, for the 1/16th bred. Just the double helix of my DNA,
my ability to sun-brown, and my own green-eyed children
of the voyageur, river visions still caught in their irises.
We're born out of a long ago season.
Everyone is sure of place and race. Blood and semen
mixed in dirt and cervix, convex and enchanted by muskrat's eerie smile,
dark truth furred and matted, stroked by a river paddle.
Let that long tooth bite now in the land of the race riots,
negro, and redskin, the underground railroad,
and the Indian village.
Let the name Pontiac take new form and hit the road,
the righteous mile where judgement and boundary blurs,
especially on matters of composition
blood, bone, and relations.

Legend/agenda

If there is no legend about the fish in Dundurn,
let this be it: when a pelican swallows a fish,
she shits the eyes onto the shore
where they turn to stare at people on the lake,
to cheer sad aluminum boats with power motors,
and asshole dads who dump beer ends, cigarette butts,
and sodium laurel sulphate into the lake while
a thousand bushes tremble a jellied weeping, suds in their ducts.
Mr. Mosquito won't you join my killing party?
You needle-snouted bastards need to make the agenda tonight
for a massacre of sucking. They're already marinated in Labatt Blue.
And those who chase the pelicans,
they're on the agenda too.

Prayer of the agnostic

All morning I dream of dogs, their nails clicking
on the hardwood floor, a pack of wanting beasts,
until I wake enough to realize
it is the rain on the roof, or a goddess' fingernails
coming to rip a hole in my house
and make a compost heap of my life.
It won't be difficult, for I've been too small,
kept fear in my pocket, but I've loved you
unselfishly. I've loved you more than myself.

I should have been wiser
to the blood-thirst of the animals. Their insatiable taste
for the insincere.

Let only my good intentions be weighted evenly
as on the scale of Anubis.

Let my good intentions count for something
when the fates come calling.

Constitution

But let's go back to a time when you were the thought of a thought
your thought was having, when you were a seed in the white striped
belly of a spider living in a glow of a window on an indigo morning
while the train clanged by and let's say you could start again in a life
where you remembered to be thankful and forgot bewilderment,
and remembered to put grass underfoot each day. Yes.
That's the spot. But let's go further than that and take back this country
from its leaders and slip back to thirty-nine cent gas, but past that too,
past treaties and rations, to a time when even Métis was good enough
to have enough to eat. Status versus mixed blood versus willow-white
French and English, and land was wider than it seems now. But let's
slip past that too, to the time of a wood frog, the time he was king
and the birds listened to his throat-song for the sake of understanding
moon time, cycles bigger than life. Yes, let's slip all the way back
to the dimpled mud home of that frog. Then let's start again. Let's teach
the spider how to have mercy for the fly, let's teach magpies not to steal
the songbird's egg, let's start with a thought. No. Let's start
with that very first thought, while it was still a thought,
before it became a thing, a noun, a country, a nation, before it became you,
before it wrapped itself in thread and became a predator, sun drenched
and glorious, sworn to its own consumption.

Oh, by the way

You were on my mind this morning
before I fully awoke,
dream still alive in the fine-grained dark.
I could see your eyes,
eyes that I could once tell time by.

You said you wasted too much of your youth
partying with me.
A few months after that
you came to my other friend's funeral, heard the eulogy
and said you hoped you could be a friend like that again.
I don't know which of your eyes to believe.
I'd call but you'd say,
you are too busy to talk.
You have been for years.
Your kids need you, just now.
Kids I've never met, though I'm sure they're in elementary school.
And you have to go and you have book club tonight
with your good friend
who lives so close,
and the wine tastes so crisp.
I am sure that's true.
I know what it's like to see
into your eyes when you laugh.

Unrequited

Scrawny-legged me, walker of a barrel-chested white dog,
lover of the weed-slicked hill in the park, mini skirts,
under-aged temptress of high school boys, their rusty cars,
and camouflaged hard-ons. You: unforgotten one.

We have such eyes for one another above the desks
in drafting class. My blood changed overnight. Your name
on my stationery: Scott tape. My ears turn towards you,
dish to satellite, sweet immaculate hope in my breast.

Sky-eyes squinty and optimistic when we took our beer
to the beach. We, a tribe of two, awkward, infatuated, inert.
Treaties were written before we touched, schools closed before
agreements were made. Mountains built. Fight or flight?

Why, I ask, a good way off in space and time,
did my feral-lust pass out on you?

Red sky at morning

Crows agree as they fight over water-bath
and beetle. Snake is the twisted stuff in a pavement crack
on the hill leading up to oblivion. Frog dwells
under pulpit of mud, keeps on preaching. Rabbit
is a fucker. Dog is a territory with a fence of teeth.
Cricket is an obstacle on the heat wavy road. Bottle picker
is an odour of beer and sugar, a tangle of hair, face a shadow
covering a little boy and what he once thought. Squirrel
is hormone. Bird is predator and parent, somehow both
and none. And you, dad, are Mahakala over me,
waving my heart in a cup with a knife for my dharma,
and somehow I, I am soft butter.

The narrative

So, Somerset Maugham, he's reading Proust in the desert. And as he's reading, he's rapt, you know? Then he does this strange thing.

He pulls the pages out of the book and flings them to the wind and sand and camels. And another man comes along, maybe the next day or a week after, I'm not sure which.

And he picks up the pages, which aren't really a story anymore–more the impression of a story with the same words and similar cadences and all the same characters.

But everything is wind tossed and rearranged, enormous leaps of strangeness, and he finds them half buried in a dune, or crumpled deep in a camel's hoof-print.

But each passage is still art, you know, language flies its way into his hair and he can't get it off his head, it's salve, a lover's breast, pleasurable, water lilies after all that sand.

Both men are equally satisfied with the experience, this way of reading: the man on the horse with his book all in order like a map or a plan, and the man behind.

He's making his own footsteps in the dune, making his way through it too, but not the way Proust intended. Which way is the best experience?

And I don't know which man I'd rather be, which is the best story.

Three dogs and an old man

Out of orchard they tumble.
Dog over dog, an undulation.
Playful, brown. First two, then another
tail, exclamation, punctuation.
A man, a silhouette, Zeus-like,
wielding his walking staff.
Creator of all things joyful and strong,
all beings four-legged and two,
he's here to say, *jubilance is a stick,*
go fetch it.

Almanac of the Douglas fir

This is me, following you up a hill, giving up on the idea of self
as one with the universe. We make two tracks here, up slope,
trees curtain what's above. I can't tell the weather
in the goddess' eye. Douglas fir. White birch. A stand
of random Mountain Ash. Trunks frame us. They say,
this is the land of the Blackfeet, and I believe heat from their fire
still burns in this grove. Ladybug. Black fly. Mosquito. Coyote.
When I was a child, dream of rabbit, dream of bear. Today,
I find you in the parking lot. It isn't a conspiracy. It's the lie
you told yourself that I see into, unbend. It's a memory of water,
the caress of the current, the frog in the creek outside my window
tapping Morse code. You slid into me, a Mobius strip, until the end
and beginning meld into one. Two sides one. On the trail, I found
bottles, trees, stones. What else have I to declare? Just a river,
running at the speed of my blood. A red squirrel
takes flight, but now it is a hummingbird.

Cormorants

Sometimes, this is your experience:
the wood frame under your fingertips,
or barnacles under your shoes. Flowers on the table, a garden
blooms out of your eyes when you sleep, and you do sleep.
You dream another life, like the last one never existed.
You gather magnolia petals, tulip petals, apple blossoms,
you forget you lived above the tree line with pine cones and scree.
The beach calls you, not the way the river's long pulse thrummed
yesterday. So much water, so much life on this shore crackles
under your footsteps. You tell the dream to your lover
in morning when sunlight simmers behind curtains,
imagine a water glass, shore-line & wave song, the cormorants,
their black diving, their rolling over in the high, wet tide.

Le deluge

—after Anne-Louis Girodet de Roussy-Trioson (1806)

Pissing rain and the Orangerie is closed,
tucked under scaffolding and smoking men.
The nearest café had shit smeared on the toilet and sink.
I make you leave before you taste your beer.
You suggest the Louvre, just over Pont Royal.
The museum exhales busloads of people shedding
odours and noises, accents and Euros, gum and photo flashes.
Inside, we wander the halls. You point at the places
you used to sit alone when you lived here,
haunting the boards on Pont des Arts above the Seine.

Vendredi, when lightning from the skylights
points at the Girodet, at inescapable fate.
You and I hold hands and watch
a movie in still life where triangles
composition, us, and desire,
where two sources of light
lash a man to a tree, and the largest storm
pulls his woman, his children, to a God-angry river.
Her cloak afire, alive. There is no hope,
but he hangs onto his hope, his woman, his lover,
until...let's say, forever.

For there are still such mysteries, and such advice

> Good poems should rage like a fire
> Burning all things, burning them with a great splendour.
> One wrapt flame at noontide bends
> The seer's inhuman stare, the seaweed's trance.
>
> —IRVING LAYTON

The rabbits in my blood have turned to circus freaks
roaming my veins looking for a place to breed.
They nibble at arterial walls that must taste
of daisies and satisfaction. Their prints atomic, toes
ionic. Their fur, my DNA. They burrow in my kidney
and have litters in my spleen. Sometimes I sleep in
all morning just to recuperate from the sounds.
I pray to Irving Layton, hope he sends a hard-on to beat back
those rampant herbivores. Something for my fingers.
He says, Good poems should rage like a fire.

What have I been eating that makes me have such
thoughts? My horoscope says, attend a sing-along.
Try more meditation. Drink lots of water. Do sit-ups
after Lent. My mother offers gardening, bird watching,
and love thy neighbour though one has thrown an axe
into her fence. The fortune teller tells me, stay limber
and away from windows, but only on Thursdays
when the moon is gibbous or waning. Such specificity!
Her lipstick sparks hellfire, and her mouth is an ember
burning all things, burning with great splendour.

I want the blue of my walls to simulate the colour of real sky.
I want to love you all. But I dislike Steven Harper.
I imagine at his centre, he tastes of the bile of a thousand
underworld toads, or that vile sour candy called "baby wipe."
My father says, give up liquor, all worldly things, and my husband.
That's quite a lot. My pancreas objects. I think I'll write to John
Wall Barger, ask for recommendations on courting the tarantula.
Sometimes, I wonder if I can do it, any of it at all.
Then I recall the time I kayaked for hours, till I had gone
to lake-end and made fire: One wrapt flame at noontime fogs

perceptions. When I meet a tree tall, dark, and thin, I'm already
sizing up sculptural form, what to set free. It's a full-time occupation,
this sorting things out. My fortune cookie says, make friends
with a man with a horse. I wish it said, hung like. Such small detail,
such different meaning. I wonder when anything will ever go
all the way my way. The astrologer says, take more chances.
It's too late, fear has already perforated me. I feel the lagomorphs
pump their flanks in my chest. Over time, oracle has shifted
from Delphi to gypsy dive, and still I seek this shoddy advice,
the seer's inhuman stare, the seaweed's trance.

Consecrated grounds

In my ignorance–there I said it–
no love with my body beyond the bounds
of this room, this bed, beyond the oneness of us.

Would you ask this of vision, periphery, or fire,
stay tight in a circle consecrated with chalk
and salt and cinder blocks?
This little round room, big as a pupil fixed.
No, not still, just untamable.

Rapid eye movement

Veils of sleep still heavy on my eyelids in the place I can still recall
    the dream: we.
We are in bed making love, my ex-student and I, the age-appropriate one,
the only one I've ever had a crush on. But wait.
He morphed then into you. You are much shorter, and a Jew.
Then you morphed again into the man I loved. The one I married,
who lives deep in changed marrow in my untamed bones, my blood.
Then you became a woman too, dark-haired and -eyed,
a certainty of hand strokes down my spine. I see all at once and perfectly,
Zeus, his shape-shift to a swan, and Leda, legs open for him,
whatever his pretty form, or lovely skin.

Ooh nom

But her name was *Oh no, not again on Monday*, and she stopped coming to class after the office appointment when he stared at her ankles and imagined them bejewelled with tiny bells, genie style. He imagined how he would trace his fingers up from those ankles and onto her back in the patterns of prayer rugs or fish scales. He'd take afternoons of time to finish infinite loops of worship. He's become a Zoroastrian and she, she would be Good.

And she asked about her essay grade, splicing his thoughts with her disruptive commas and insufficient logic. She wore Converse, black, no laces, no socks. He knew she was dating the tallest boy in class with the nose ring, his yoga body, his Dharmsala recollections from his gap year, building thunderheads of dreams and desires from which she could attach, then detach.

But he thought of how close he'd come last week in the student lounge on wing-Wednesday when the pub-students asked him, and they did, who his student crush was and her name was on his tongue like a devotion, a benediction, a supplication, and when he raised his hand he called out, *Stella Artois*.

And he called her *Oh no, not again on Monday*, which when shortened sounded like Ooh nom. He dreamed of her earlobes, sacraments between his lips. He'd skim her like a float-plane full of survivalist supplies and diamonds.

But she waved his own rubric at him, threatening, bewildered. And his penis, mortified, defensive, ready to espouse him, his outlines, twitched and ready to comfort her, rose in solidarity.

And what he meant to say was, "I'll allow you to rewrite," but his tongue rebelled, still lucid and tangled in mantras and bed-sheets said, "Will you allow me to bite?"

Then her face unfurled like a thousand Persian knots, retied themselves tight as a flock of starlings. And from their wings came an orgasmic hum that flew into the hallway fast as her scream.

About suffering

> And ghosts must do again / What gives them pain.
>
> —AUDEN

Distracted by *A Whiter Shade* and heading into traffic,
I don't see the point, brain, in remembering all that shame
right fucking now. The groceries are condensing all over
themselves as a muddy minivan swerves to avoid my car.
All I see are fingers. Birds. Flipping. I'd like to be home
basting garlic and taking notes on my ideal day.
I haven't written a poem about you, now, for 432 days.
432 days without accident. Without that killing floor.
I can't remember your face anymore without thinking
of all the decisions I made, that made us into being
all three of us. No, make that four. I almost forgot your wife.
About suffering, Auden is a clairvoyant and never wrong.

If you

gaze at the stars, they turn their fiery irises
towards our wet/dirty planet and watch the tidal
motion of person piercing person
with penis, and gladius, and bullet.

A supergiant's own combustion
sparks light, honesty.
We merely chalk compassion
on blackboards, speak it from pulpits
without much purchase for permanence.

If you speak, remember, speech is the symbolic act
of a reasonable citizen. The white star turns back to itself,
silent when faced with this glut of gibberish and babble.
Its heart is dense with so much bad news.

If you stare into the abyss, the abyss stares back
and the stars too,
but then they must blink,
turn away: indifferent.
They must–
having no hands to help or heal.

No snow falls

until the moon is deep towards
the sun's turning to longer days.
A full month late, this November.
Things shift when the neighbour moves
his Corvette parked under the willow for the last twenty years.
The slow rotation of the tires flick rust into the driveway, distracts
squirrels from their fits of mating.
The back alley neighbour no longer
putters out to open the garage door. We all turn towards
solitude. Anxiety keeps on,
a ticking drone speaking out of the doomsday clock.
No doubt, change is in the air, its breath is on my neck.
Sparrows still commit themselves to windows,
outraged occupiers bang their wings into dark districts.

I like the way
things will go on without us,
without all I could point to and say,
here is my home, these are the landmarks, this is my almanac.

Pupil

Listen, a child knows a green secret, a wilderness born from a clump of dirt. Every child's heart knows it moulds that universe with spatula and thumb. Let's change the shape of trees by willing them to follow. Close your eyes, feel the roots twisting into feet. Even now, I tell you a story. Lean in. Speak this with all sincerity. The secret is simple; it's all in the tone. Make an O with your mouth. Make your irises hum as though the bones of your skull are the very origin story. Feel silence centre, ripple out, orbit. Go back to the start. Learn to make a new world come.

How to be in a garden

—for J.K.

> From this newly turned earth,
> Every tip of me gathers under your touch,
> Wind wrapping my dress around our legs,
> Your shirt twisting to flowers in my fists.
> —ANNE MICHAELS

I'd already packed all winter clothes in my suitcase
for the wrong season, the frogs were already at mating,
another type of sunlight caressed the buds. Spring.
How was I to know I had been lying to my body? What next?
Repack or ignore my miscalculations? How many secrets
can I keep from my own arteries under my hunched shoulders?
Do I want to know the species of that bloom or wear a down
vest while everyone else is sun-bathing? It's hard not to notice
the one covered lady on the beach in noon-day heat
when from this newly turned earth, so much pushes up,

out towards the sun and the bees. Feel that pressure
after the night's chill? Ants crawl up peonies.
Hummingbirds complain to koi. By the pond,
a stone heron promises the moon to frogspawn.
I need a knife to cut through all this bullshit.
You are in your kitchen doing taxes, making potatoes
for dinner tonight. And we've sent 89 texts today
professing our love. The Japanese maples don't care. I fell
asleep under your spell and awoke as if you were in the room.
Every tip of me gathers under your touch.

You're just what I need: sugar-water in the feeder.
I'd pray for this change of season again. It's not your fault.
I love you now that I've take into account
how quickly weather shifts. I wasted too much time.
I'm not supposed to be writing love poems to you.
I can't seem to pacify this desire you've lit in me.
Even a distracted mind can read this outward radiance.
They predict a change in precipitation, but all I feel is heat
and the wind wrapping my dress around our legs.

You can't be here fast enough, inside me. It's been a long time
since I've felt that dam burst. Watch out, little villagers downstream.
Ferns will unfurl, giant and lush in this monsoon year.
You can't put that cat back in the bag.
Little wildheart, hollow out a body-shaped nest.
I wear a blue ring to mimic the sky in my veins
since you asked me to leave my guilt in the road.
Did you know, you made a sound when we met?
It sounded like yum. Since then, I've gone to blossom
with your shirt twisting to flowers in my fist.

Fleece

All night, Salman Rushdie chastised me in my dreams
at a cocktail party with blushing martinis and authors
deep as carpet tuft. This happens to me often.
His nametag said Dr. Authenticity. It's hard
to be an atheist in this valley, to wake from that sort of sleep.
I would agree even the shore seems god-lit. This morning
seems like a reason as good as any to make off like a loon,
spear some breakfast and fly out to the middle of the lake,
break from my self-inflicted insanity.

Thorn apples

The other day, when I was counting up all the things
I'd done and said and made possible for you,
I passed a florist in the mall, a window of flowers,
a thorn apple, a flora bomb, and I thought

of the things I'd done and said and made possible for you,
of all the times you forgot to say thank you, took me for granted,
a floral, naval bomb exploded in me and I thought
of how you dismissed me as irrelevant,

of all the times you forgot to say thank you, took me for granted,
and I wanted to make a bouquet for you
dismiss it as irrelevant afterthought,
deceitful charms, Janus fruit.

And I wanted to make a bouquet for you.
I thought, for a moment, of shoving them
those deceitful charms, those Janus fruit,
up your nose.

I thought of shoving them,
with my raw knuckles,
up your nose,
this fist full of spikes.

Dust

It takes four minutes to steep a presse coffee. I want to be in love
with the world, with goths, hipsters, and chic, slick ladies in their
Free People jeans. My cordless blue telephone isn't built the same
as the scene with Marilyn Monroe, tragic, naked, and drugged.
The world shifts, twists in wireless jibber-jabber. I thought I could afford
a five-star hotel after twenty-seven years of correcting verb forms and
adjectives. A certain kind of forgetfulness is useful when starting new
projects and re-evaluations. Maybe the Buddhists already knew
this meditation. Incantations and Carl Sagan say we are star-stuff
and astonishment, from the same dust. I hope you realize
what this means. I fall in love with many things, and all at once.
Have you come up against that heart-birth? The wind has seduced
my ears and clover and rabbits have bloomed in my eyes.
Their wild irises the last light I will ever see before I go to seed. I hope
you realize what I meant when I said it's time to let go; I hope
you realize what I meant when I said, it's me, not you.

Another day of feminist perspective

And it has been said you should be more charming,
that no one wants to hear what you have to say,
that you should not name the elephant in the corner.

And it should also be said you have not been tamed,
that you should not believe the eyes that have seen you as small,
though they squint narrow with fear

wrapped as doubt, slit wise and black, turn to pupils
who set the track high-bar that you will leap in the distance as a hurdle,
and you will load the springs in your legs and fly into the future,

earning your keep, your children's manners, your place at the helm
while still believing in meritocracy, and monogamous true love's kiss.
Maybe someday you will be brave enough to say aloud,

when asked: Who are you? Maybe then
you will loosen your grip on it all, say,
I am nothing, and I, too, I am all things.

Relativity

I wonder if all existence is you and I, our other selves, doppelgangers,
other lovers, in all afternoons, with spring's new light streaming
through tall pines and windows. The she you once told me about who
riveted him to tears in his eighties in his cottage after a confession
that you betrayed because I understood so well. I do mean she of course,
and him, and you, I mean he, you said it because I, I mean she already
exposed everything to you. She lay down bare, and stupid, and soft,
and let him in, and the she, the she is me, the me who disappeared after
that scene at the sea, no the she was him, and we, we are like them too,
only worse, and where are you now? I can't imagine, he can't imagine,
you can't imagine where I've gone, where she's gone, after all these letters
here like predators still wanting order and love and sunlight. And each of us
is on our chairs, right now, right then. I was rubbing your calf, no she
was rubbing his calf, and he was rubbing hers too and neither could stop
smiling, because, just then, they were becoming all the people they wanted
to be, in that moment, but that was a while ago, although,
it seems like just yesterday.

Reasons for learning cursive

Index finger traces your name in bathwater.
You've penned it on my breast, my back,

you've traced and tagged me wherever bare skin
lies, and in places too small for your lengthy moniker,

you slant your scrawl, spin letter on letter as if stacked
dip, shaft, list, you spell and loop, straighten, sign.

Hand on quim, roll and ripple up, I
scribble where your fingers trace again.

Compose under water, on my body, hot
slick ink, put it in writing, label me yours, and
when I sigh your monogram, pen it again, mark me indelibly.

I always wanted a tattoo

> In the end I would rather wonder than know.
> I never got my tattoo, and never will.
> I hesitated too long, and the time in which one acquires such
> things passed, as all things will.
>
> —MARY RUEFLE

Of a flock of birds winding up around my hip
and across my belly, up and over my shoulder,
between my breasts, up my neck like a spiral
or a corkscrew. I saw a hummingbird chase
a squirrel in a pine tree up that path, a skirmish
with beak and claw, tooth versus wing,
a tiff that came to no blood. Just the chitter and squawk
of two fools marking territory in a space
big enough to hold them both. In the end
I would rather wonder than know

where the territory lines stop and start
and live reckless by crossing those
paradoxical borders of earth, water, and air.
Have you ever leaned down in sand,
squinted at a shore-line eye to eye? It's not a line,
but a shimmer, a wave, a blur, impossible
to ink with damselfly, or magnum needle,
enduring without permanence or stasis.
Borders shift and move, whirl.
I never got my tattoo, and never will.

I still admire the tree, its certainty of freedom,
belonging to neither bird nor mammal.
No citizenship to blood. Life rocks
on past this feeble quibble.
For what is it to attach to the small dramas
of one season's nesting beasts? Much
more comes in the letting and the going.
Root keeps on rooting.
Cone keeps on seeding.
I hesitated too long, and the time in which one acquires such

wisdom has already cost me half my life.
Entropy claims the natural order of things.
Tree is the best mentor, but even
a trunk turns to driftwood
in time. I have already talked
myself out of a tattoo. Indelibly
marking myself no longer
matters. *Always* isn't real to me, wanting
is now about contentment, essentials.
Now, I simply notice things pass,
as all things will.

Of appreciation

I see you, Don McKay, russet clad
in a parka, pushing a cart at the Co-op.
Who would have thought that you too

need groceries after all the lichen and birdsong
that sustains you? I thought you lived on airy stuff
after that hike on Tunnel Mountain when you still had shoes,

before your feet turned to claw. I watch you for a while,
flit about the produce bins where you morph into a wood-pecker
to the harmony of Muzak. All that red still in your wings,

your toes turn to tarsus, clutch a fat pineapple. You deliver
it to the eleven items or less till. And I think it improbable,
the weight of that bark-covered fruit, your tiny beak,

your geometric crest, all that heavy juice. I thought
you were impossible. I remember when, on the mountain, you saw all
that was invisible in the rock seam, in that north rock. Incredible

the flight-path of the magic-eyed in their own element.
But, when you bagged your own fruit with those claws,
even customer service gave you a low whistle of appreciation.

Self portrait at 2:45 am

Somehow in this impossible room
I've become part of a sing-along
in a group of writers at a quarter to
fuck-it's-late. What do I do now to exit this space?
The old lady in my hip complains. My bed needs
a sleep mate. It's obvious. This will never happen
again. Across the sofa, a boy half my age.
His bulky pockets shadow a night from twenty-five
years ago, when embered lust's heat
learned, *I love you*, meant,
you made me cum ten times, when amazement
in each others' eyes meant spliffs and sex all night
on basement waterbeds. I can honestly say, now,
I know peace of mind, and though less sleep
deprived, yet more sure I am loveable and wise.
Still, something majestic in the boy's khakis
speaks of happiness, bulbous, unattainable, wild
as it is from this place and time, yet still
sifted by the same amazed moonlight.

Firewall

Some say pagans of the post-modern
experiment with consciousness
using caffeine and YouTube videos of Ram Dass.
They flirt with firewalls on Silk Road.
Now, there's some old-fashioned hippy bullshit with home delivery.
I don't believe the women with glass throats still live,
or call the moon down into their salted circles,

but there is something in the water tonight, a certain sympathy,
a certain remembrance of night-smoke and pheromones.
Remember, there in the darkened room?
Would I know where to hide from you now? If you had a pitchfork,
and I was the hunted.

Who is the blamer?
Who is the blamed in this pursuit, or any for that matter?
Oh, don't worry, we'll get through this.

Some say women of the twenty-first century don't know how to grow old,
or wise. But, let me tell you, I know the crow-song when I walk,
I knew the language from birth, claimed my right to hear it.
How about you, bluster-man? What lives in your marrow?
Will you meet me in the park, near the water? How about the valley?
Do you want to call me baby? Or hold me in your hands like a fetish?
Do you want me to write the coda?
How about a drink?

If an answer lives on your tongue,
let's define the words: good woman.
But just for tonight.

Inclement

Birds have flown into my ears
made my skull a faraday cage.

What of you sweet swimmer,
bathing in the hurricane?

What of my love for you?
I hear you packed for the Island

last week. I hear you make
for redemption. It's not on the map.

I want to believe all the sparks
I feel. This body is a liar.

You are a village that I once
plundered when I was a band of Vikings.

If I left you in flames, then be a phoenix,
rise up from whatever remains.

Dive

Some nights, I see your body,
age-bent, a hedgehog in silhouette–
not the way you used to be,
when I knew you intimately.

I wait all night for your voice
to float me up off the bed
into starfish shapes, weightless,
undulating, the light
in all of my cells harmonized.
A hum I can't forget. It sounds like
regret, regret, regret.

It's an old story, this one, a sea-girl
in love with a land-boy.

My sheets, so heavy this morning.
Yet they feel like home,
then falling.

Evacuation

Everything is swollen with its own pulse.
Even the floating three-leaf clovers,
heads just above the accumulating puddle,
battle surface tension for a last
glimmer of air before the step-down stream
trickles them perfectly under.

A friend is leaving rocks at the anchor of a bridge,
one at a time, *an old Jewish tradition*, she says,
to mark your visit to the dead.
I pick a pretty, banded rock today,
throw it away. I have too many rocks to stack.

Back in the big city, sandbags resist
the mighty Bow, its banks a-roil
with debris, stone-age weaponry,
a highway that will not let me pass.
I bought a bright thing for you today,
red as a scar, thin as a butterfly.

Here, I want you to have it, in the hallway
of dicey weather and hopeful cleanser.
Why is it so easy to detect the covered up?
There's a jag in the riverbank now
where the water wanted through, a new bank,
all those wrenched, naked roots.

Mercurial

Another tidal rain falls
between street and sky,
the wash of years between us
scrawled and heavy in my pockets.

The weight of that note slips
under the press of your body on mine,
that indelible surrender
your crowning penis.

I have no way now
of telling you
the most obvious things
though I've held nothing back.

How I wish this grey would morph
into something mythic. A carrier pigeon perhaps.

Citizenship of the broken heart

Not one of us leaves unscathed.
All stories tainted by degrees of disaster.
Pick a lucky number.

Yesterday, I met a man with an angry scar
across his cheek, a machete bite,
a blessing, a station of the cross to bear.

And here is a story of the elephant described by two blind men–
this a tusk, this an ear. Calculus and compassion
have much in common when counted on fingers.

In this line-up of catastrophe,
we all have a number, we'll all be called
and sworn into suffering, sometime.

Fear of water

Water took my breath and kept it for its own.
It had its task, to seek its own level.

When I fell into my father's sister's pool, when
my sputtering stopped and my eyes went yellow,
there was a dog on the lawn, a haze in the sky.
My father's hand snagged the back of my collar and pulled me out
until I remembered air. I don't recall his being there,
only the chill of my clothes and the puddle on the car seat while
    going home,
all the hell I was catching.

I've saved his life, too. One dawn, I heard him in the bathroom.
Pneumonia taloned his lung. I already awake and listening, roused
by some angel who needed a hasty substitute. I'd already dialled 911
when he cracked open his skull and perception,
when he almost drifted off to that place he can't forget.
He doesn't remember me that morning
                                        just all the beautiful nothing he felt.

Is it love, I wonder?

That vicious haul
    back to life like that?

The chosen

—for Basma

A girl I know walks outside in dusk, where I wouldn't dare
for fear of cold and ticks, or ghosts in the road.
She knows her way by feel in moonlight,
she knows the way because the owl tells her where to go.

This divination of feather and talon is her fate,
because she takes herself outside, feels the shiver in the air
when he comes divining down, wings wide, grey horns high.

She does not flinch when he comes for her,
does not fuss with small details:
no earth under her feet.

Let free

If I compare this morning to any morning,
then what about the clarity of yesterday when
it all went spectacular. Therefore,
tree, grass leaf, what does seed matter?
They take no struggle in their difference,
nor expectation. Grass does not expect to become
a tree, so let free. And let free the lovers, too–
their mystery, duality in union. Blindfolded Eros,
his arrowed alchemical blend on his bowman's tool.
The world opens to new priorities: a straight shot through.
Let free intention, let free triumph, let me master
the Sphinx after the desert spits him out. Let me choose
the clear path, progress mine for the taking,
when the onus of power shifts. Let free,
I am victory. I spread my wings. I cover much ground.

Ordinary days

After I saw the snake skiff over
the pavement like water on a hot skillet
I began to worry about my luck.

Oblivious until your pointed index finger
turned that perceived stick to tragic opera
of mouth and mouse, of strangle and swallow.

Snake was on the move and the mouse
butt end, feet a-dangle, was stiffed. I don't need to upload
this National Geographic scene.

Mostly, I need to comment on luck,
yours specifically, how it's a full flush,
a very good hand. I could have lived

a thousand years with the same sets of days
and never been dealt what gives itself
so naturally to you.

Drop of doom

At the country fair, you ask, what will become of us when we are old?
You tell me of dreams, of wheelchair races, of the grandfather
who makes you crazy with his senile whims.

In this life we love what we will.

You rail against his automobile; you've confiscated the keys.
You ask me if I would have done the same.

Who am I to know?
Perhaps I'll sit in a blue Lotus when I am ninety-two,
wear Aviators, yell vroom-vroom.

Keats asked us to know comfort in the unknown thing,
negative capability, to accept the unexpected pealings of Chiron's bell:
one friend died of a heart attack, another leukaemia, a third, a stroke.

At the fair I would never ride the Drop of Doom.
Yet, here we are on that very thing,
without line-up, without ticket, being elevatored up.

We can't possibly know how or when the floor will drop out,
or if some variety of god will save us.

Our worlds, routines, and bodies only half known
all of the time. *Dimitium notum.*

What is certain is never certain.
Are you listening to the only question that matters?

Who am I, when I have no answers?

We’re already on our way.
Can you see outer space above the tiny parking lot?

There is no place that does not see you

—after Rilke

Yesterday, no trees demanded insight from me.
And they won't again today. Therefore, I walk
among them again. Much of life insists,
even small things demand responsibility:
the water bottle commands recycle, melody requests repeat,
even lungs drum time to breath. I weary of this beauty,
but there is no place that does not see you.

The Algonquin make violation of keeping:
bannock always breaks. Greed means obscenity,
and ownership disease. Notice now that lung again,
how villi release, ventilate carbon back to trees.

We're all in symbiosis here.
We'll all emancipate our molecules back.
How complicated is that?

Between the trees

—for Reid

You've already invented fifteen ways to die, separated into five acts
dramatized for our supper company. But let me tell you, son. I've
seen death sneak, really sneak, between the trees, slim as a fawn and
quick as an eye. And I made a pact when you were born. So I chase
him through scattered leaves and nip through narrow paths and
ferocious shrubbery. Follow me, and find me, son, hand-in-hand with
you, flying skyward on the amusement ride. I've spied him there
above the pine, and shallow reeds making for the shore.
He's in the skin of lake, pike-slick and under hull. He slinked among
the sheep in France, morphed into a baby goat who ate your shoelace
at the zoo. Did you know you were that close when he nipped behind
the pony barn? And on that zip-line in Montana, did you sense the tang
of iron in the air as we gathered speed before he fled and camouflaged
himself as just another date on the calendar. I see him all the time,
flicker-quick, an early bat, a swooning moth that eats days and weeks
and years. Don't forget, he's looking for us too. And if I catch him first,
remember, in all that blue between the trees, I am in full flight, full flung,
chasing him down for you.

Talisman pool

In another fragment of your childhood, son, you attend lessons for jumping off high boards at the pool, your need for adrenalin apparent since babyhood. One day playing airplane, you laughingly head-butted my eye black and for three weeks. I explained to strangers, *it wasn't domestic,* while pointing at your baby-fuzz head, your toothless smirk, half expecting belief, even then you had that laugh.

Today, waterside, you perform a Cleese-esque demo of silly walks instead of the jumping-jacks you've been asked to do, your hand in the air waving across to me asking, "Are you looking at me, mom, can you see?"

Son, I promise you, I haven't blinked.
I've been staring all your life.

I've forgotten more than I knew

The most obvious things surprise me
when I've waited for love.

My memory is origami paper
double-sided, blank / decorated.

Suddenly I remember the entirety of an argument on ethical living
while standing near the coffee pot, but can't find my keys.

There's a secret inside me I never knew but will tell you
in firelight with enough pinot gris.

Memory is not a recording device.
The core of me is kind.

I re-invent all the ways I could have done things better,
all those I've left behind,

all the love I could have made,
but was too bewildered to try.

Free

The dogs in my brain run amok.
Random thoughts hopped up on caffeine
bark up skull walls. Doubt echoes
curse   blessing   curse
from the abyss shouted into,
reverberating between thought and feel. Fear
in the heart of a canine needs a taming.

Little savage, little wildheart, hush your growling snarl-tooth.
Nothing lives in the ghost-spooked air
but sparrows and relief.

Benediction

—after Seamus Heaney and Jane Munro

do not be afraid
do not be afraid
embrace the unknown,
noli timere, noli timere,
om mani padme hum,
noli timere, noli timere,
alpha, omega, locapala, om,
dark matter quintessence
noli timere, noli timere,
mudras of the vajras, Zeus,
seven stars, nine gates of destiny,
noli timere, noli timere,

noli timere, noli timere,
do not be afraid
do not be afraid

I bet you already knew

I broke up, once, like mercury dispersed, bearings out from the mother drop, a solid thing diffused, whole, but not quite whole. An elegant biology of molecules orbited out from the centre of the thing called self, called existence. It happened at a lake. I paddled out to the horizon between glacial scour and outer space. I faced up, or was it down? Either way promised untouchable infinity.

There's something to be said for that kind of silence.

I floated until my mind was empty of human words, until it existed in *feel*, only in *feel*, beyond the abilities of this poem, its inept syllables, until I knew my own smallness in the universe. Then came the tingling, the dispersal, the love, not the love of a man or woman, nor mother or father, but the love, the big thing, the big we, the big other, maybe infinity. But let's not rush to name it. Let's not spoil it with that.

You know what I mean.

Cells peeled, one by one, like electrons off a nucleus, separate but held. The space between–the ancients called ether, quintessence, a highway for light and gravity. And at the centre was ball of white, a fifth element, and all the things I'd ever done badly or wrong didn't matter, but all the feel concentrated, intensified, a storm of stillness and explosion. Simultaneous. Beyond body, beyond self. Do I explain this thing, this coming apart as oneness? Does that make sense?

Are you still with me, after all this otherworldly talk?

Time unhinged was unknown. This feel lasted for maybe a second, maybe an afternoon. Does it matter how long? What matters is that it happened at all. And somehow, it has become infinite, for I can recall it now, that burst into twinkling. Have you ever felt like that? When everything and nothing matters, but

love.

Acknowledgements

My gracious thanks to Bill Bunn, Lauren Carter, The Electronic Garrett, George Elliott Clarke, Rosemary Griebel, Richard Harrison, Steven Heighton, Basma Kavanagh, Jeff Kovitz, Patrick Lane, Ross Maylor, Shelley McAneeley, Natalie Meisner, Peter Midgley, Susan Plett, Kirk Ramdath, Sharanpal Ruprai, Juleta Severson-Baker, Joan Shillington, Tara-Dawn Solheim, and Jan Zwicky.

Some of these poems were published in *CV2*, *Eco-Echo Poetics*, *Fiddlehead*, *Wax*. This manuscript was shortlisted for the Matrix Robert Kroetsch Innovative Poetry Award. Thanks to the Alberta Foundation for the Arts for their generous support of this project.

I can't wait to go in reverse, to make the things in the world exist again, one by one, or all together.

—ITALO CALVINO

Other Titles from The University of Alberta Press

Demeter Goes Skydiving

SUSAN McCASLIN

Award-winning poet exercises the profound mother-daughter trauma forged in the Demeter-Persephone myth with unapologetic modernity.

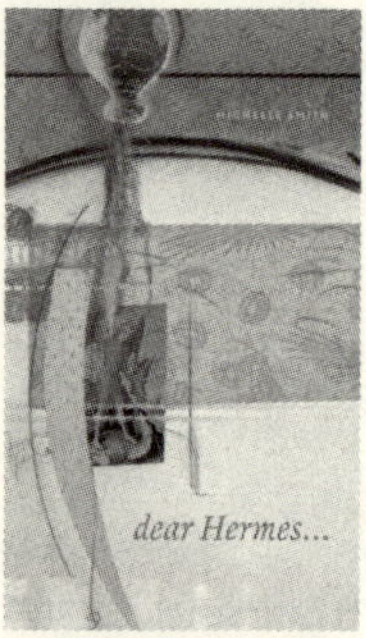

dear Hermes...

MICHELLE SMITH

This Canadian Prairie poet's debut collection is framed by imaginative travelogues addressed to Greek gods.

Trying Again to Stop Time

Selected Poems

JALAL BARZANJI

Dream-like cadences of international landscapes, human desire, and visions of a loving and wounded poet.